D1442082

Native Americans

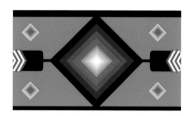

Shawnee

Barbara A. Gray-Kanatiiosh

ABDO Publishing Company

visit us at
www.abdopub.com

Published by ABDO Publishing Company, 4940 Viking Drive, Suite 622, Edina, Minnesota 55435. Copyright © 2004 by Abdo Consulting Group, Inc. International copyrights reserved in all countries. No part of this book may be reproduced in any form without written permission from the publisher.

Printed in the United States.

Cover Photo: Corbis
Interior Photos: AP/Wide World pp. 28, 29; Corbis pp. 4, 30
Illustrations: David Kanietakeron Fadden pp. 7, 9, 11, 13, 15, 17, 19, 21, 23, 25, 27
Editors: Kate A. Conley, Jennifer R. Krueger, Kristin Van Cleaf
Art Direction & Maps: Neil Klinepier

Library of Congress Cataloging-in-Publication Data

Gray-Kanatiiosh, Barbara A., 1963-
    Shawnee / Barbara A. Gray (Kanatiiosh)
        p. cm. -- (Native Americans. Set III)
    Includes index.
    Summary: An introduction to the history, social structure, customs, and present life of the Shawnee Indians.
    ISBN 1-57765-938-4
    1. Shawnee Indians--History. 2. Shawnee Indians--Social life and customs. [1.Shawnee Indians. 2. Indians of North America--East (U.S.)] I. Title. II. Native Americans (Edina, Minn.). Set III.

E99.S35G7 2003
974.004'973--dc21

                                                      2002033000

About the Author: Barbara A. Gray-Kanatiiosh, JD
Barbara Gray-Kanatiiosh, JD, Ph.D. ABD, is an Akwesasne Mohawk. She resides at the Mohawk Nation and is of the Wolf Clan. She has a Juris Doctorate from Arizona State University, where she was one of the first recipients of ASU's special certificate in Indian Law. Barbara's Ph.D. is in Justice Studies at ASU. She is currently working on her dissertation, which concerns the impacts of environmental injustice on indigenous culture. Barbara works hard to educate children about Native Americans through her writing and Web site, where children may ask questions and receive a written response about the Haudenosaunee culture. The Web site is: www.peace4turtleisland.org

About the Illustrator: David Kanietakeron Fadden
David Kanietakeron Fadden is a member of the Akwesasne Mohawk Wolf Clan. His work has appeared in publications such as *Akwesasne Notes*, *Indian Time*, and the *Northeast Indian Quarterly*. Examples of his work have also appeared in various publications of the Six Nations Indian Museum in Onchiota, NY. His work has also appeared in "How the West Was Lost: Always the Enemy," produced by Gannett Production, which appeared on the Discovery Channel. David's work has been exhibited in Albany, NY; the Lake Placid Center for the Arts; Centre Strathearn in Montreal, Quebec; North Country Community College in Saranac Lake, NY; Paul Smith's College in Paul Smiths, NY; and at the Unison Arts & Learning Center in New Paltz, NY.

Contents

Where They Lived

The Shawnee homelands were located in what is now the northeastern United States. They lived east of the Mississippi River, along rivers such as the Cumberland and the Ohio. Their territory included parts of present-day Ohio, Tennessee, Kentucky, Virginia, and Pennsylvania.

The Shawnee homelands were beautiful. These lands held forested mountains, hills, valleys, and grasslands. Colorful wildflowers and flowering trees and shrubs covered the land. There were also lakes, streams, and ponds filled with fish, muskrat, and beavers, as well as many types of birds.

The Cumberland River runs through a forest in Tennessee.

The Shawnee spoke a language in the Algonquian language family. They lived south of other Algonquian-speaking nations. In fact, the word *Shawnee* comes from an Algonquian word meaning "southerners." The Shawnee's neighbors included the Huron, Iroquois, Delaware, Kickapoo, and Miami tribes.

Shawnee Homelands

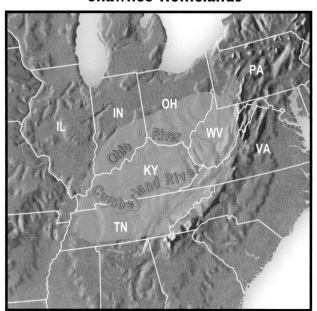

Society

The Shawnee built their villages along rivers. The rivers provided the Shawnee water to drink and food to eat. In addition, the rivers provided protection. For example, Shawnee villagers could use a river for a quick getaway when hostile people approached. For added protection, the Shawnee sometimes built a **palisade** around each village.

About 300 people lived in each Shawnee village. Originally, the Shawnee had 12 clans. Some of these clans were the Turtle, Wolf, Beaver, Panther, and Deer. The Shawnee were cared for by medicine people. These healers knew how to prepare herbs, wildflowers, tree bark, and other plants to cure illnesses.

Each village also had a peace chief and a war chief. Peace chiefs were responsible for setting up and performing ceremonies. War chiefs had the responsibility of protecting the village from hostile people. The chiefs worked together to plan hunting and fishing trips. They also acted as judges when villagers wronged each other.

A Shawnee village

Food

    The Shawnee produced their own food. They hunted, fished, and gardened. They also gathered wild plants. Some of the plants they gathered were wild leeks, berries, nuts, and herbs.

    Shawnee men hunted with bows and arrows and flint-tipped spears. For meat, they hunted elks, bison, and deer. They also set snares to catch rabbits, squirrels, beavers, ducks, and geese.

    Shawnee men fished for bass, walleye, catfish, pike, perch, and muskellunge. To catch the fish, the men used spears and a hook and line. Before the Shawnee first met Europeans, they fished with forked spears carved from wood. After meeting Europeans, the spearheads were usually made of metal.

    Shawnee women grew corn, beans, squashes, and sunflowers. The Shawnee ate many of the crops while they were still fresh. But, they also dried some vegetables, meat, fish, and wild plants in the sun and saved them to eat during the winter. Ripe corn was dried and ground into **meal**. The meal could be used to make corn bread or mush.

The Shawnee held seasonal ceremonies related to food. The green corn ceremony gave thanks to the corn. The whole village came together for the event. During the ceremony, the Shawnee took green corn off the cob and made it into soup. The whole village ate the soup, gave thanks, danced, and sang.

A Shawnee man readies his bow and arrow while hunting elk.

Homes

The Shawnee made their homes from natural materials. They had two common types of homes. They built dome-shaped wigwams and rectangular bark houses.

To begin building a wigwam, Shawnee men first dug a pit 12 inches (30 cm) deep. This pit served as the floor. Next, they buried the ends of sapling poles in the ground. They bent the tops of the poles over the pit to form a dome-shaped frame. The men tied the poles together with rope made from plant fibers.

Once the frame was built, the women covered it with animal hides, bark, or mats woven from cattail reeds. Sometimes, they used a combination of materials. They left a hole open in the roof to allow fire smoke to escape. An opening was left in the side for a door.

The second type of home was a bark house. This house was similar to an Iroquois longhouse, except it was not as long. A Shawnee bark house began with a frame of sapling poles. Next, the men covered the frame with either birch or elm bark. They then tied cross poles to the frame to hold the bark in place. In the roof, they left a smoke hole.

Both types of homes had doors of either woven mats or animal hides. Inside, the Shawnee made beds by covering branches with hides or fur robes. On hunting trips, the men lived in temporary shelters made from animal hides stretched over a few poles, similar to a lean-to.

1 To make a wigwam, the Shawnee first set up a frame of poles.

2 Next, they covered the frame with bark, hide, or woven mats.

3 Last, they secured the bark with more poles. The door was covered by a woven mat or animal hide.

Clothing

Women made the Shawnee's clothing. They sewed with bone needles and thread rolled from plant fibers or animal **sinew**. They made the clothes with plant fibers or deer, elk, or bison hides. Once done, the women decorated the clothing with porcupine **quillwork** or paint.

Men's clothing consisted of animal-skin **breechcloths** and moccasins. They also wrapped sashes and belts around their bodies. In addition, they wore waist- or thigh-high **leggings**. The leggings protected the men's legs from brush and thorns.

On their heads, Shawnee men wore turbans or wide headbands. They often decorated the turbans with a feather. Feathers from eagles, hawks, and owls were highly regarded.

Women's clothing was usually deerskin dresses and moccasins. They also wore animal hides and skirts, as well as mantles woven from plant fibers. These mantles tied around the neck and hung down to the top of the skirt. In cold weather, both men and women wore fur robes to keep warm.

A woman and man dressed in typical Shawnee clothing

13

Crafts

The Shawnee were skilled craftspeople. One common craft was making birch bark containers. They used bark because its inner layers are very strong. To begin, the Shawnee used stone, bone, or antler tools to cut strips of bark from a tree.

Next, they soaked the strips in water to make the bark soft and flexible. This made it easier to form the bark into a container. Then, the Shawnee cut the bark and bent it to form bowls, plates, baskets, and other containers. Finally, they punched holes into the sides and sewed the pieces of bark together with spruce roots.

Besides making bark containers, the Shawnee also carved. To prepare, they first took maple or oak **burls** and heated them in a fire. Heating the burls made them easier to carve. Then, they carved the burls into bowls and cups.

The Shawnee also made pottery. Their pots had round bottoms and sturdy, ridged necks. They carved a simple design of straight lines into the ridged tops of the pots. People hung the pots over the fire to heat water and cook soups and stews.

A Shawnee man collects birch bark for use in crafts and homes.

Family

   Shawnee villages were made up of extended families. Family members worked together to feed and protect the people of the village.

   Every family member helped with the daily chores. The Shawnee gathered wild berries, greens, sunflowers, and medicinal plants. In addition, they collected hickory nuts and walnuts. The Shawnee also gathered some plants to make natural dyes.

   Shawnee women tended the gardens. They used hickory-handled hoes to clear away weeds. The Shawnee planted corn, beans, pumpkins, and melons. While the people worked, Shawnee elders helped watch the children. They also taught the children by telling them stories.

Men fished the rivers, lakes, and streams. Shawnee men also went on hunting trips. Sometimes they traveled great distances to find bison herds on the prairie. When they returned, the men built drying racks. The women cut strips of fish or meat and hung them on a rack to dry. Sometimes they placed the rack over a fire to smoke the meats.

Children sit with a Shawnee elder to hear stories.

Children

   The Shawnee loved their children. After a baby's birth, a Shawnee family named their child during a special naming ceremony. The parents chose the name from the father's clan. Babies were carried on **cradleboards**.

   Shawnee children loved to play games. They played ball games and ran and swam. Girls often played with dolls made of hides and natural fibers.

   Shawnee children also had a great knowledge of nature. Shawnee territory was home to poisonous snakes, including cottonmouths and timber rattlesnakes. The Shawnee taught their young children how to identify and avoid these dangerous snakes.

   Boys and girls learned by helping with daily village tasks. They helped gather wild berries and plants. Boys learned how to make stone, bone, and antler tools. They watched as the men chipped away stone to make spears and arrowheads.

Shawnee girls helped the women plant and weed the gardens. The girls also learned how to make clothing. They practiced by sewing dresses and tiny moccasins for their dolls.

A man teaches a Shawnee boy how to make tools.

Myths

    Every Native American nation has its own creation story. These stories tell how the people came to this world. The following is a Shawnee creation story.

    A long time ago, there was no planet Earth. There was only a Sky World, and beneath this world was nothing but clouds and water. One day Kuhkoomtheyna, "Our Grandmother," left Sky World. She sat on a cloud and created a giant sea turtle. She placed the sea turtle in the water.

    Next, Kuhkoomtheyna began to create the earth. Cloud Boy, her grandson, and Little Dog watched. She made streams, rivers, mountains, valleys, meadows, and lakes. She also made trees, birds, and animals.

    Kuhkoomtheyna placed the earth, which looked like a giant ball, on the turtle's back. Then she created her grandchildren, the Shawnee and other peoples. She gave the Shawnee fire and medicine bundles, and taught them ceremonial dances and songs.

Cloud Boy is a jokester. Sometimes he changes clouds to look like animals, or he hides articles of clothing. The next time you see a cloud in the sky that looks like an animal, think of Cloud Boy, Little Dog, and Kuhkoomtheyna.

Cloud Boy and Little Dog watch as Kuhkoomtheyna creates the earth.

War

The Shawnee often had to fight to protect themselves. They fought against many Native American nations, including the Erie, Neutral, and Iroquois. Planning how to launch an attack on the enemy was the job of the war chiefs. The chiefs also trained the young warriors.

In warfare, the Shawnee fought with bows and arrows. For close combat, they used stone, bone, or antler knives. They also fought with war clubs. The Shawnee made both ball and root war clubs.

The Shawnee crafted root war clubs from the root close to a sapling tree. They carved the knobby roots to make them sharp. Ball war clubs were made using a **burl** from a maple or oak tree. The men attached handles carved from ironwood trees to the burl. Sometimes they embedded a tooth or arrowhead in the burl. This made the war club even more deadly.

After the Shawnee began trading with Europeans, warfare became even deadlier. That's because the Shawnee were able to obtain guns as well as metal knives and arrowheads. But, many enemy tribes received these goods before the Shawnee. As a result, many Shawnee were killed, and those remaining were driven to new lands.

A Shawnee warrior holds a ball war club, a bow, and arrows.

23

Contact with Europeans

The Shawnee's early contact with Europeans was friendly. In 1541, Spanish explorer Hernando de Soto and his party were the first Europeans to see the Mississippi River, in present-day Tennessee. At this time, it is believed that de Soto met a band of Shawnee.

In the late 1600s, French explorer René-Robert de La Salle explored the Ohio region and the Mississippi River. Some of this land was Shawnee territory. At one point, one of his men joined and lived with a band of Shawnee.

In the early 1770s, Europeans threatened Shawnee territory. Lord Dunmore, governor of the British colony of Virginia, claimed lands belonging to the Shawnee. Soon traders and settlers began to move into these areas. Some Shawnee launched raids against the settlers.

Lord Dunmore sent troops to keep order. So, Shawnee chief Cornstalk led a **rebellion** against the British. This fight is known as Lord Dunmore's War. The Shawnee were defeated and signed a peace treaty.

During the American Revolution, the Shawnee fought with the British against the colonists. The Shawnee sided with the British to stop the American colonists from settling in their territory. In 1795, the Shawnee and other tribes signed the Treaty of Greenville with the United States. This treaty caused the Shawnee to lose a lot of their original homelands.

Hernando de Soto meets a Shawnee man.

Tecumseh & the Prophet

Tecumseh (tuh-KUHM-suh) was a respected Shawnee leader. He was born in about 1768 in present-day Ohio. The name *Tecumseh* means "Panther Springing Across the Sky." He had a brother named Tenskwatawa, who was known as the Prophet.

Tecumseh and his brother worked hard to protect the Shawnee people. The Prophet warned the Shawnee to avoid alcohol and told them to protect their traditional way of life. Tecumseh was also a great **orator**. He visited with other Native American nations to talk about his vision to protect native people.

At this time, it was common for individuals to sell lands that did not belong to them. Tecumseh and the Prophet wanted the people to agree that land could not be sold without approval from all of the Native nations. Tecumseh said that if the nations united, they could stop the loss of land and **culture** due to the expansion of the United States into the West.

During the War of 1812, Tecumseh fought on the side of the British. It was his hope that the British would stop the settlers from invading Shawnee lands. Tecumseh died at the Battle of Thames on October 5, 1813, in present-day Ontario, Canada.

Tecumseh is one of the best-known Native American leaders.

The Shawnee Today

In 1830, the U.S. government created the Indian Removal Act. The purpose of the act was to remove Native American tribes from their homelands and relocate them west of the Mississippi River. The Shawnee were forced to leave their homelands for Kansas. Eventually, the U.S. government relocated the Shawnee to present-day Oklahoma.

Today, there are three **federally recognized** Shawnee reservations. They are the Absentee Shawnee, the Eastern Shawnee, and the Loyal Shawnee. All three reservations are located in Oklahoma.

Hawk Pope is chief of the Shawnee Nation United Remnant Band in Ohio. There are three federally recognized Shawnee bands, but the United Remnant Band is only recognized by Ohio's state government.

The Absentee Shawnee consist of the Big Jim Band and the White Turkey Band. They have an elected government and an Elder's Council. The Elder's Council plans social activities.

Shawnee official Jim Great Elk Waters visits the 200-year celebration of the Lewis and Clark Expedition at Monticello, the home of Thomas Jefferson.

The Eastern Shawnee tribe is working to improve the lives of its members. For example, it is working on a housing development for its members, and it promotes Eastern Shawnee businesses. Recently, the tribe built a bingo hall and casino.

The Loyal Shawnee lived within the Cherokee Nation for more than 130 years. During this time, they sought state and **federal recognition**. They finally received it in 2000. The Loyal Shawnee can now govern their people directly, without having to go through the Cherokee government.

The Shawnee are working hard to preserve their language and **culture**. As a part of this preservation, they hold traditional ceremonial dances. Bread dances are held in the spring and fall. The spring dance gives thanks and asks for good crops. The fall dance asks for good hunting.

In the summer, the Shawnee hold green corn ceremonies to give thanks. Some Shawnee also hold buffalo dances. These dances honor those who have fought in war.

Shawnee John Gibson dresses in ceremonial clothing for a festival.

Glossary

breechcloth - a piece of hide or cloth, usually worn by men, that wraps between the legs and ties with a belt around the waist.

burl - a hard, rounded woody growth on a tree.

cradleboard - a flat board used to hold a baby. It could be carried on the mother's back or hung from a tree so that the baby could see what was going on.

culture - the customs, arts, and tools of a nation or people at a certain time.

federal recognition - the U.S. government's recognition of a tribe as being an independent nation. The tribe is then eligible for special funding and for protection of its reservation lands.

leggings - coverings for the legs, usually made of cloth or leather.

meal - coarsely ground seeds.

orator - a public speaker noted for skill and power in speaking.

palisade - a fence of strong stakes placed closely together and set firmly into the ground.

quillwork - the use of porcupine quills to make designs on clothing or cradleboards.

rebellion - an armed resistance or defiance of a government.

sinew - a band of tough fibers that joins a muscle to a bone.

Web Sites

To learn more about the Shawnee, visit ABDO Publishing Company on the World Wide Web at **www.abdopub.com**. Web sites about the Shawnee are featured on our Book Links page. These links are routinely monitored and updated to provide the most current information available.

Index